MW01006233

A

POCKET

DICTIONARY

OF THE

VULGAR TONGUE

A CAVEAT FOR

COMMON
CURSETORS,

VULGARLY CALLED

VAGABONES

a dictionary of
BUCKISH SLANG,
UNIVERSITY WIT,
AND PICKPOCKET
ELOQUENCE

———

A BOOK
VERY USEFUL
AND NECESSARY
[*to be known, but not practiced*]
FOR ALL PEOPLE

A POCKET DICTIONARY OF THE

VULGAR TONGUE

AN ABRIDGMENT OF
*A Classical Dictionary
of the Vulgar Tongue*

BY Captain Francis Grose
EDITED BY Steve Mockus
ILLUSTRATIONS BY Johnny Sampson

CHRONICLE BOOKS
SAN FRANCISCO

A BRIEF
INTRODUCTION

First published in 1785, *A Classical Dictionary of the Vulgar Tongue* is one of the first lexicons of English slang, compiled by the artist, militia captain, and antiquarian [and by one account "the greatest porter-drinker of his day"] Francis Grose. It collects terms he overheard on late-night excursions in search of adventure through London's slums, dockyards, and taverns—anywhere that, according to his contemporary British writer Pierce Egan, "a 'bit of life' could be seen to advantage, or the 'knowledge-box' of the Captain obtain anything like a 'new light' respecting mankind, he felt himself happy, and did not think this time misapplied. It was from these nocturnal sallies, and the slang expressions which continually assailed his ears, that Captain Grose was first induced to compile *A Classical Dictionary of the Vulgar Tongue*."

Grose describes the dictionary as drawing from "Cant Language" [basically, criminal lingo], as well as "burlesque terms . . . drawn from the most classical authorities; such as soldiers on the long march, seamen at the capstern, ladies disposing of their fish, and the colloquies of a Gravesend boat." He also collected terms while witnessing executions. Inspired by a French satirical and burlesque dictionary, he felt the English language deserved its own, and pointed to the freedom of thought and speech riding along with such wit.

The dictionary as a whole is invaluable as a cultural record, and notable for the many terms therein that Grose collected as colorful that are still with us today [for example, "birthday suit" for nakedness], some of which I've included at the end here. But many other of the thousands of words and phrases he collected have fallen into disuse, which is a shame. This selection is primarily culled from the 1796 edition [revised and released a number of times, the 1796 edition is the last that Grose oversaw, according to philologist and lexicographer Eric Partridge]. It is meant be a LARK, fun and useful—pocket sized, and ready to add a little flair to conversations, or to wield in unfortunate encounters with ADDLE PATES.

Still in Use Today

—

AGAINST THE GRAIN

APRIL FOOL

BABBLE

BAMBOOZLE

BATTLE-ROYAL

BIRDS OF A FEATHER

BIRTHDAY SUIT

BOLLOCKS

BRAT

CAT CALL

CHAP

DILDO

ELBOW GREASE

ELBOW ROOM

FART

FLOUT

GLIB

GLUM

HELTER SKELTER

HOCUS POCUS

HODGE PODGE

HONEY MOON

HUSH MONEY

JAIL BIRD

JILTED

KICK THE BUCKET

KINGDOM COME

LAME DUCK

LINGO

LOUT

NICKNAME

OAF

PRICK

QUOTA

RANDY

RASCAL

RIFF RAFF

SANDWICH

SHAG

SHAM

SHEEPISH

SHIP SHAPE

SHOPLIFTER

SLANG

SNITCH

SNIVEL

SNOOZE

SNUB

SMUT

A POCKET
DICTIONARY
OF THE
VULGAR
TONGUE

A.

ACCOUNTS. To cast up one's accounts;
to vomit.

ACTIVE CITIZEN. A louse.

ADDLE PATE. An inconsiderate foolish fellow.

ADMIRAL OF THE NARROW
SEAS. One who from drunkenness

vomits into the lap of the person sitting opposite to him.

ALTITUDES. The man is in his altitudes, *i.e.*, he is drunk.

ANCHOR. Bring your a-se to an anchor, *i.e.*, sit down.

ANKLE. A girl who is got with child, is said to have sprained her ankle.

APPLE DUMPLIN SHOP. A woman's bosom.

ARBOR VITÆ. A man's penis.

ARS MUSICA. The backside. *See* BUM-FIDDLE.

The Backside

ARS MUSICA

BLIND CUPID

BUM-FIDDLE

DOUBLE JUGG
[MALE]

B.

BACK GAMMON PLAYER. A sodomite.

BACON. He has saved his bacon; he has escaped. He has a good voice to beg bacon; a saying in ridicule of a bad voice.

BAG OF NAILS. He squints like a bag of nails, *i.e.*, his eyes are directed as many ways as the points of a bag of nails.

BALSAM. Money.

BAPTIZED, or CHRISTENED. Rum, brandy, or any other spirits, that have been lowered with water.

BARBER'S SIGN. A standing pole and two wash balls.

BARKING IRONS. Pistols, from their explosion resembling the bow-wow or barking of a dog.

BARNACLE. A good job, or snack easily got.

BARREL FEVER. He died of the barrel fever; he killed himself by drinking.

BASKET-MAKING. The good old trade of basket-making; copulation, or making feet for children's stockings.

PLATE I

Basket-making

BATCH. We had a pretty batch of it last night; we had a hearty dose of liquor. Batch originally means the whole quantity of bread baked at one time in an oven.

BAWBELS, OR BAWBLES. Trinkets; a man's testicles.

BEAR-GARDEN JAW. Rude, vulgar language such as was used at the bear-garden.

BEARD SPLITTER. A man much given to wenching.

BEAST. To drink like a beast, *i.e.,* only when thirsty.

BEAST WITH TWO BACKS. A man and woman in the act of copulation.

BEAU TRAP. A loose stone in a pavement, under which water lodges, and on being trod upon, squirts it up, to the great damage of white stockings; also a sharper neatly dressed, lying in wait for raw country squires.

BED. Put to bed with a mattock, and tucked up with a spade; said of one that is dead and buried. You will go up a ladder to bed, *i.e.*, you will be hanged.

BEDFORDSHIRE. I am for Bedfordshire, *i.e.*, for going to bed.

BEEF. To cry beef; to give the alarm. They have cried beef on us. To be in a man's beef; to wound him with a sword. To be in a woman's beef; to have carnal knowledge of her.

BEGGAR MAKER. A publican, or ale-house keeper.

BEGGAR'S BULLETS. Stones. The beggar's bullets began to fly, *i.e.*, they began to throw stones.

BELCH. All sorts of beer; that liquor being apt to cause eructation.

BETWATTLED. Surprised, confounded, out of one's senses; also bewrayed.

BEVERAGE. Garnish money, or money for drink, demanded of anyone having a new suit of clothes.

BIRD-WITTED. Inconsiderate, thoughtless, easily imposed on.

Money

BALSAM

BEVERAGE

BIT

BLUNT

CARAVAN

CHUMMAGE

CLY

COD

COLE

CORIANDER
SEEDS

CRAP

CROP

DARBY

DUST

IRON

KING'S
PICTURES

MUCK

PLATE

QUIDS

RAG

RHINO

RIBBIN

SPANKERS

SPANKS

STEPHEN

BIT. Money. He grappled the cull's bit; he seized the man's money. A bit is also the smallest coin in Jamaica, equal to about sixpence sterling.

BITE. A cheat; also a woman's privities. The cull wapt the mort's bite; the fellow enjoyed the wench heartily.

BLANKET HORNPIPE. The amorous congress.

BLIND CUPID. The backside.

BLINDMAN'S HOLIDAY. Night, darkness.

BLOW. He has bit the blow, *i.e.*, he has stolen the goods.

TO BLOW THE GROUNSILS. To lie with a woman on the floor.

BLUBBER. The mouth. I have stopped the cull's blubber; I have stopped the fellow's mouth, meant either by gagging or murdering him.

BLUE RUIN. Gin. Blue ribband; gin. *See* **RIBBIN.**

BLUE TAPE, OR SKY BLUE. Gin.

BLUNT. Money.

BOB. A shoplifter's assistant, or one that receives and carries off stolen goods. All is bob; all is safe.

BOBBED. Cheated, tricked, disappointed.

BONE BOX. The mouth. Shut your bone box; shut your mouth.

BONES. Dice.

BOTTLE-HEADED. Void of wit.

TO BOX THE JESUIT, AND GET COCK ROACHES. A sea term for masturbation; a crime, it is said, much practised by the reverend fathers of that society.

BRACKET-FACED. Ugly, hard-featured.

BREAD BASKET. The stomach; a term used by boxers. I took him a punch in his bread basket; *i.e.*, I gave him a blow in the stomach.

BREAK-TEETH WORDS. Hard words, difficult to pronounce.

PLATE II

Bufe Nabber

BREAKING SHINS. Borrowing money; perhaps from the figurative operation being, like the real one, extremely disagreeable to the patient.

BREECHES. To wear the breeches; a woman who governs her husband is said to wear the breeches.

BROWN MADAM, OR MISS BROWN. The monosyllable. *See* MONOSYLLABLE.

BUB. Strong beer.

TO BUBBLE. To cheat.

BUFE. A dog. Bufe's nob; a dog's head.

BUFE NABBER. A dog stealer.

BUFF. All in buff; stript to the skin, stark naked.

BUFFLE-HEADED. Confused, stupid.

BUG-HUNTER. An upholsterer.

BUM-FIDDLE. The backside, the breech. *See* ARS MUSICA.

BUN. A common name for a rabbit, also for the monosyllable. To touch bun for luck; a practice observed among sailors going on a cruize.

BUNG UPWARDS. Said of a person lying on his face.

BURN CRUST. A jocular name for a baker.

BUSHEL BUBBY. A full breasted woman.

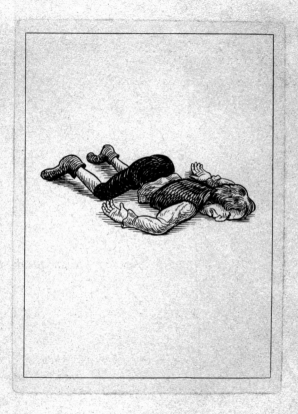

PLATE III

Bung Upwards

BUTCHER'S DOG. To be like a butcher's dog, *i.e.*, lie by the beef without touching it; a simile often applicable to married men.

BUTTOCK BALL. The amorous congress.

BUTTOCK BROKER. A bawd, or match-maker.

C.

CABBAGE. When the scrotum is relaxed or whiffled, it is said they will not cabbage.

CACAFUEGO. A sh-te-fire, a furious braggadocio or bully huff.

CACKLING CHEATS. Fowls.

CACKLING FARTS. Eggs.

PLATE IV

Cackling Farts

CANDY. Drunk.

CANNISTER. The head. To mill his cannister; to break his head.

CAPTAIN HACKUM. A blustering bully.

CARAVAN. A large sum of money.

TO CASCADE. To vomit.

CASTING UP ONE'S ACCOUNTS. Vomiting.

TO CAT, OR SHOOT THE CAT. To vomit from drunkenness.

CAT LAP. Tea, called also scandal broth. *See* SCANDAL BROTH.

CAT-HEADS. A woman's breasts.

CATCH FART. A footboy; so called from such servants commonly following close behind their master or mistress.

CAUDGE-PAWED. Left-handed.

CHATTER BROTH. Tea. *See* CAT LAP and SCANDAL BROTH.

CHEESE IT; BE SILENT, BE QUIET, DON'T DO IT. Cheese it, the coves are fly; be silent, the people understand our discourse.

CHEESE-TOASTER. A sword.

CHEESER. A strong smelling fart.

CHICKEN-HAMMED. Persons whose legs and thighs are bent or archward outwards.

PLATE V

Cat-heads

CHIRPING MERRY. Exhilarated with liquor. Chirping glass, a cheerful glass, that makes the company chirp like birds in spring.

CHITTERLINS. The bowels. There is a rumpus among my bowels, *i.e.*, I have the colic.

CHITTY-FACED. Baby-faced; said of one who has a childish look.

CHOAKING PYE, or COLD PYE. A punishment inflicted on any person sleeping in company: it consists in wrapping up cotton in a case or tube of paper, setting it on fire, and directing the smoke up the nostrils of the sleeper.

CHOPPING. Lusty. A chopping boy or girl.

TO CHOUSE. To cheat or trick: he choused me out of it. Chouse is also the term for a game like chuck-farthing.

CHUCKLE-HEADED. Stupid, thick-headed.

CHUMMAGE. Money.

CHURCH WORK. Said of any work that advances slowly.

CHURCHYARD COUGH. A cough that is likely to terminate in death.

CIRCUMBENDIBUS. A round-about way, or story. He took such a circumbendibus; he took such a circuit.

PLATE VI

Clammed

CLAMMED. Starved.

CLANKER. A great lie.

CLAPPER. The tongue of a bell, and figuratively of a man or woman.

CLAPPER CLAW. To scold, to abuse, or claw off with the tongue.

CLEAR. Very drunk. The cull is clear, let's bite him; the fellow is very drunk, let's cheat him.

CLEAVER. One that will cleave; used of a forward or wanton woman.

CLICKET. Copulation of foxes; and thence used, in a canting sense, for that of men and women: as, The cull and the mort are at clicket in the dyke; the man and woman are copulating in the ditch.

CLOTH MARKET. He is just come from the cloth market, *i.e.*, from between the sheets, he is just risen from bed.

CLOUT. A blow. I'll give you a clout on your jolly nob; I'll give you a blow on your head. It also means a handkerchief.

CLUNCH. An awkward clownish fellow.

CLY. Money; also a pocket. He has filed the cly; he has picked a pocket.

COBBLERS PUNCH. Treacle, vinegar, gin, and water.

COCK ALLEY OR COCK LANE. The private parts of a woman.

COCK-A-WHOOP. Elevated, in high-spirits, transported with joy.

COCKSHUT TIME. The evening, when fowls go to roost.

COD. A cod of money: a good sum of money.

CODS. The scrotum.

COFFEE HOUSE. A necessary house. To make a coffee-house of a woman's ****; to go in and out and spend nothing.

COLD IRON. A sword, or any other weapon for cutting or stabbing. I gave him two inches of cold iron into his beef.

COLD PIG. To give cold pig is a punishment inflicted on sluggards who lie too long in bed: it consists in pulling off all the bed clothes from them, and throwing cold water upon them.

COLE. Money.

COMFORTABLE IMPORTANCE. A wife.

COMMODITY. A woman's commodity; the private parts of a modest woman, and the public parts of a prostitute.

CONTENT. The cull's content; the man is past complaining: a saying of a person murdered for resisting the robbers.

CONVENIENT. A mistress.

CORIANDER, or CORIANDER SEEDS. Money.

CORK-BRAINED. Light-headed, foolish.

CORNED. Drunk.

CORPORAL. To mount a corporal and four: to be guilty of onanism: the thumb is the corporal, the four fingers the privates.

CORPORATION. A large belly. He has a glorious corporation; he has a very prominent belly.

COSTARD. The head. I'll smite your costard; I'll give you a knock on the head.

COVE. A man, a fellow, a rogue. The cove was bit; the rogue was outwitted. The cove has bit the cole; the rogue has got the money.

COW JUICE. Milk.

COW'S THUMB. Done to a cow's thumb; done exactly.

Onanism

———

BOXING
THE JESUIT

FRIGGING

MOUNTING
A CORPORAL
AND FOUR

TOSSING OFF

CRAB SHELLS. Shoes.

TO CRACK. To boast or brag; also to break. I cracked his napper; I broke his head.

CRANK. Gin and water; also, brisk, pert.

CRAP, OR CROP. Money.

CRASHING CHEATS. Teeth.

CREAM-POT LOVE. Such as young fellows pretend to dairymaids, to get cream and other good things from them.

CREEPERS. Gentlemen's companions, lice.

CRINKUM CRANKUM. A woman's commodity.

CROAKER. One who is always fore-telling some accident or misfortune: an allusion to the croaking of a raven, supposed ominous.

CROP THE CONJUROR. Jeering appellation for one with short hair.

CROP. Money. *See* **CRAP.**

CROPSICK. Sickness in the stomach, arising from drunkenness.

CUCUMBERS. Taylors, who are jocularly said to subsist, during the summer, chiefly on cucumbers.

CULL. A man, honest or otherwise. A bob cull; a good-natured, quiet fellow.

CUP OF THE CREATURE. A cup of good liquor.

PLATE VII

Cucumbers

CUP-SHOT. Drunk.

CUPBOARD LOVE. Pretended love to the cook, or any other person, for the sake of a meal. My guts cry cupboard; *i.e.*, I am hungry.

CURTAIN LECTURE. A woman who scolds her husband when in bed, is said to read him a curtain lecture.

CUT. Drunk. A little cut over the head; slightly intoxicated. To cut; to leave a person or company. To cut up well; to die rich.

D.

DADDLES. Hands. Tip us your daddle; give me your hand.

DAIRY. A woman's breasts, particularly one that gives suck. She sported her dairy; she pulled out her breast.

DARBY. Ready money.

PLATE VIII

Dicked in the Nob

DAY LIGHTS. Eyes. To darken his day lights, or sew up his sees; to close up a man's eyes in boxing.

DEAD MEN. Empty bottles.

DEVIL'S BOOKS. Cards.

DEW BEATERS. Feet.

DEWITTED. Torn to pieces by a mob, as that great statesman John de Wit was in Holland, anno 1672.

DICKED IN THE NOB. Silly. Crazed.

DIDDEYS. A woman's breasts or bubbies.

DIDDLE. Gin.

TO DIDDLE. To cheat. To defraud. The cull diddled me out of my dearee; the fellow robbed me of my sweetheart.

DIMBER. Pretty. A dimber cove; a pretty fellow. Dimber mort; a pretty wench.

DISGUISED. Drunk.

DO. To do any one; to rob or cheat him.

TO DOCK. To lie with a woman.

DOCTORS. Loaded dice, that will run but two or three chances. They put the doctors upon him; they cheated him with loaded dice.

DOG'S SOUP. Rain water.

DOODLE SACK. A bagpipe. Also the private parts of a woman.

DOUBLE JUGG. A man's backside.

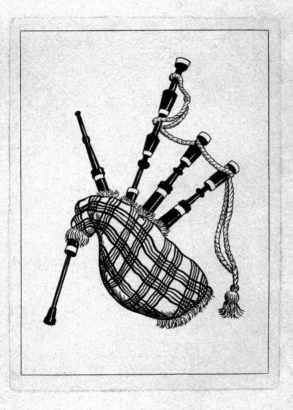

PLATE IX

Doodle Sack

D R A I N. Gin: so called from the diuretic qualities imputed to that liquor.

D R O P I N T H E E Y E. Almost drunk.

D R U N K. Drunk as a wheel-barrow.

D R Y B O B. A smart repartee; also copulation without emission.

D R Y B O O T S. A sly humorous fellow.

D U B T H E J I G G E R. Open the door.

D U C K F-C K-R. The man who has the care of the poultry on board a ship of war.

D U C K L E G S. Short legs.

D U D S. Clothes.

D U G S. A woman's breasts.

DUKE OF LIMBS. A tall, awkward, ill-made fellow.

DUNAKER. A stealer of cows and calves.

DUNEGAN. A privy. A water closet.

DURHAM MAN. Knocker kneed, he grinds mustard with his knees: Durham is famous for its mustard.

DUST. Money. Down with your dust; deposit the money. Dust it away; drink about.

E.

EARTH BATH. A grave.

EASY. Make the cull easy or quiet; gag or kill him. As easy as pissing the bed.

EMPEROR. Drunk as an emperor, *i.e.*, ten times as drunk as a lord.

ENSIGN BEARER. A drunken man, who looks red in the face, or hoists his colours in his drink.

EQUIPT. Rich; also, having new clothes. Well equipt; full of money, or well dressed. The cull equipped me with a brace of meggs; the gentleman furnished me with a couple of guineas.

ETERNITY BOX. A coffin.

EVANS. Mrs Evans; a name frequently given to a she cat; owing, it is said, to a witch of the name Evans, who frequently assumed the appearance of a cat.

EVE'S CUSTOM-HOUSE. Where Adam made his first entry. The monosyllable.

EXECUTION DAY. Washing day.

Female Naughty Bits: Below

BEEF

BITE

BROWN MADAM

BUN

COCK ALLEY

COMMODITY

CRINKUM
CRANKUM

DOODLE SACK

EVE'S
CUSTOM-HOUSE

FRUITFUL VINE

GIGG

MADGE

MAN TRAP

MISS BROWN

MISS LAYCOCK

MONOSYLLABLE

MOSSY FACE

MOTHER OF
ALL SAINTS

MOTHER OF
ALL SOULS

MOTHER OF
ST. PATRICK

MUFF

MUTTON

NOTCH

OLD HAT

PITCHER

TUZZY-MUZZY

WARE

F.

FACE-MAKING. Begetting children.
To face it out; to persist in a falsity. No
face but his own: a saying of one who has
no money in his pocket or no court cards
in his hand.

FACER. A bumper, a glass so full as to
leave no room for the lip.

FALLALLS. Ornaments, chiefly women's, such as ribands, necklaces, &c.

FAM LAY. Going into a goldsmith's shop, under pretence of buying a wedding ring, and palming one or two, by daubing the hand with some viscous matter.

FAMBLES, OR FAMS. Hands. Famble cheats; rings or gloves.

TO FAMGRASP. To shake hands: figuratively, to agree or make up a difference. Famgrasp the cove; shake hands with the fellow.

FAMILY OF LOVE. Lewd women; also, a religious sect.

FAMILY MAN. A thief or receiver of stolen goods.

PLATE X

Fambles

FANCY MAN. A man kept by a lady for secret services.

FART. He has let a brewer's fart, grains and all; said of one who has bewrayed his breeches. I dare not trust my a-se with a fart: said by a person troubled with a looseness.

FART CATCHER. A valet or footman, from his walking behind his master or mistress.

FARTING CRACKERS. Breeches.

TO FEATHER ONE'S NEST. To enrich one's self.

FEEDER. A spoon. To nab the feeder; to steal a spoon.

FEET. To make feet for children's stockings; to beget children. An officer of feet; a jocular title for an officer of infantry. *See* BASKET-MAKING.

FELLOW COMMONER. An empty bottle: so called at the university of Cambridge, where fellow commoners are not in general considered as over full of learning. At Oxford an empty bottle is called a gentleman commoner for the same reason.

FIDDLE FADDLE. Trifling discourse, nonsense. A mere fiddle faddle fellow; a trifler.

FIGDEAN. To kill.

FIN. An arm. A one finned fellow; a man who has lost an arm.

TO FIRE A SLUG. To drink a dram.

FIRE PRIGGERS. Villains who rob at fires under pretence of assisting in removing the goods.

FIRE SHOVEL. He or she when young, was fed with a fire shovel; a saying of persons with wide mouths.

FIZZLE. An escape backward. *See* CHEESER.

FLABAGASTED. Confounded.

FLASH KEN. A house that harbours thieves.

TO FLASH THE HASH. To vomit.

FLAT COCK. A female.

FLATT. A foolish fellow.

FLAWD. Drunk.

TO FLAY, or FLEA, THE FOX. To vomit.

FLICKER. A drinking glass.

FLICKERING. Grinning or laughing in a man's face.

FLOURISH. To take a flourish; to enjoy a woman in a hasty manner, to take a flyer. *See* **FLYER**.

FLUSTERED. Drunk.

FLYER. To take a flyer; to enjoy a woman with her clothes on, or without going to bed.

FLYERS. Shoes.

FOOL FINDER. A bailiff.

Drunk

CANDY

CHIRPING MERRY

CLEAR

CORNED

CUP-SHOT

CUT

DISGUISED

FLAWD

FLUSTERED

FOXED

FUDDLED

HICKSIUS DOXIUS

IN HIS ALTITUDES

IN THE GUN

IN THE SUN

MAULED

NAZY

POGY

SWALLOWED A HARE

WRAPT UP IN
WARM FLANNEL

FOREFOOT, or PAW. Give us your fore foot; give us your hand.

FOREMAN OF THE JURY. One who engrosses all the talk to himself, or speaks for the rest of the company.

FOUL. To foul a plate with a man, to take a dinner with him.

FOXED. Intoxicated.

FREEHOLDER. He whose wife accompanies him to the alehouse.

FRENCH LEAVE. To take French leave; to go off without taking leave of the company: a saying frequently applied to persons who have run away from their creditors.

PLATE XI

Frog's Wine

TO FRIG. To be guilty of the crime of self-pollution.

FRIG PIG. A trifling, fiddle faddle fellow.

FROG'S WINE. Gin.

FRUITFUL VINE. A woman's private parts, *i.e.*, that has flowers every month, and bears fruit in nine months.

FUDDLE. Drunk. This is rum fuddle; this is excellent tipple, or drink. Fuddle; drunk. Fuddle cap; a drunkard.

FUDGE. Nonsense.

FUN. A cheat, or trick. Do you think to fun me out of it? Do you think to cheat me? Also the breech, perhaps from being the abbreviation of fundament. I'll kick your fun.

G.

GALLIGASKINS. Breeches.

GAYING INSTRUMENT. The penis.

GENTLE CRAFT. The art of shoe-making. One of the gentle craft: a shoemaker: so called because once practised by St. Crispin.

GENTLEMAN COMMONER. An empty bottle; a university joke,

gentlemen commoners not being deemed over full of learning.

GENTLEMAN OF THREE INS.
In debt, in gaol, and in danger of remaining there for life: or, in gaol, indicted, and in danger of being hanged in chains.

GENTLEMAN OF THREE OUTS.
That is, without money, without wit, and without manners: some add another out, *i.e.*, without credit.

GENTLEMAN'S COMPANION.
A louse.

GENTLEMAN'S MASTER. A
highway robber, because he makes a gentleman obey his commands, *i.e.*, stand and deliver.

GIB CAT. A northern name for a he cat, there commonly called Gilbert.

GIBLETS. To join giblets; said of a man and woman who cohabit as husband and wife, without being married; also to copulate.

GIFT OF THE GAB. A facility of speech.

GIFTS. Small white specks under the finger nails, said to portend gifts or presents. A stingy man is said to be as full of gifts as a brazen horse of his farts.

GIGG. A nose. Snitchel his gigg; fillip his nose. Grunter's gigg; a hog's snout. Gigg is also a high one-horse chaise, and a woman's privities. To gigg a Smithfield hank; to hamstring an over-drove ox, vulgarly called a mad bullock.

GILLS. The cheeks. To look rosy about the gills; to have a fresh complexion. To look merry about the gills: to appear cheerful.

GINGAMBOBS. Toys, bawbles; also a man's privities. *See* THINGAMABOBS.

GLIM. A candle, or dark lantern, used in housebreaking; also fire. To glim; to burn in the hand.

GLIMMS. Eyes.

GLUEPOT. A parson: from joining men and women together in matrimony.

GNARLER. A little dog that by his barking alarms the family when any person is breaking into the house.

GOAT. A lascivious person. Goat's jig; making the beast with two backs, copulation.

GOGGLES. Eyes. *See* OGLES. Goggle eyes: large prominent eyes. To goggle; to stare.

GOLLUMPUS. A large, clumsy fellow.

TO GRABBLE. To seize. To grabble the bit; to seize any one's money.

TO GREASE. To bribe. To grease a man in the fist; to bribe him.

GREEN GOWN. To give a girl a green gown; to tumble her on the grass.

GRINDERS. Teeth. Gooseberry grinder; the breech. Ask bogey, the gooseberry grinder; ask mine a-se.

GROPERS. Blind men; also midwives.

GRUMBLE. To grumble in the gizzard; to murmur or repine. He grumbled like a bear with a sore head.

GRUMBLETONIAN. A discontented person; one who is always railing at the times or ministry.

GRUTS. Tea.

GULL. A simple credulous fellow, easily cheated.

GUM. Abusive language. Come, let us have no more of your gum.

GUN. He is in the gun; he is drunk: perhaps from an allusion to a vessel called a gun, used for ale in the universities.

GUT SCRAPER, or TORMENTOR OF CATGUT. A fiddler.

GUTS. My great guts are ready to eat my little ones; my guts begin to think my throat's cut; my guts curse my teeth: all expressions signifying the party is extremely hungry.

GUTTER LANE. The throat, the swallow, the red lane. *See* RED LANE.

GUZZLE GUTS. One greedy of liquor.

H.

HAIR SPLITTER. A man's yard.

HALF SEAS OVER. Almost drunk.

HAMS, or HAMCASES. Breeches.

TO HANG AN ARSE. To hang back, to hesitate.

HARD AT HIS ARSE. Close after him.

Male Naughty Bits:
The One

ARBOR VITÆ

HAIR SPLITTER

PEGO

PLUG TAIL

SILENT FLUTE

SUGAR STICK

THOMAS

TICKLE TAIL

HARE. He has swallowed a hare; he is drunk; more probably a *hair*, which requires washing down.

HARUM SCARUM. He was running harum scarum; said of any one running or walking hastily, and in a hurry, after they know not what.

HASH. To flash the hash; to vomit.

HAT. Old hat; a woman's privities: because frequently felt.

HEAD RAILS. Teeth.

HEARING CHEATS. Ears.

HEART'S EASE. Gin.

TO HEAVE. To rob. To heave a case; to rob a house. To heave a bough; to rob a booth.

PLATE XII

Heart's Ease

HEAVER. The breast.

HERRING POND. The sea. To cross the herring pond at the king's expence; to be transported.

HERTFORDSHIRE KINDNESS. Drinking twice to the same person.

HICKEY. Tipsey; quasi, hickupping.

HICKSIUS DOXIUS. Drunk.

HIGGLEDY PIGGLEDY. Confusedly mixed.

HIGH EATING. To eat skylarks in a garret.

HIGH ROPES. To be on the high ropes; to be in a passion.

HIGH SHOON, OR CLOUTED SHOON. A country clown.

HIGH WATER. It is high water, with him; he is full of money.

HISTORY OF THE FOUR KINGS, OR CHILD'S BEST GUIDE TO THE GALLOWS. A pack of cards. He studies the history of the four kings assiduously; he plays much at cards.

HOCKS. A vulgar appellation for the feet. You have left the marks of your dirty hocks on my clean stairs; a frequent complaint from a mop squeezer to a footman.

HODDY DODDY, ALL A-SE AND NO BODY. A short clumsy person, either male or female.

HOG GRUBBER. A mean stingy fellow.

HONEST WOMAN. To marry a woman with whom one has cohabitated as a mistress, is termed, making an honest woman of her.

HOOD-WINKED. Blindfolded by a handkerchief, or other ligature, bound over the eyes.

TO HOP THE TWIG. To run away.

HOP-O-MY-THUMB. A diminutive person, man or woman. She was such a hop-o-my thumb, that a pigeon, sitting on her shoulder, might pick a pea out of her a-se.

HOPPER-ARSED. Having large projecting buttocks: from their resemblance to a small basket, called a hopper or hoppet, worn by husbandmen for containing seed corn, when they sow the land.

HORN COLIC. A temporary priapism.

HORSE'S MEAL. A meal without drinking.

HUBBLE-BUBBLE. Confusion. A hubble-bubble fellow; a man of confused ideas, or one thick of speech, whose words sound like water bubbling out of a bottle.

HUMP. To hump; once a fashionable word for copulation.

HUMPTY DUMPTY. A little humpty dumpty man or woman; a short clumsy person of either sex: also ale boiled with brandy.

I.

ICE, or FOYSE. A small windy escape backwards, more obvious to the nose than ears; frequently by old ladies charged on their lap-dogs. *See* FIZZLE.

IDEA POT. The knowledge box, the head. *See* KNOWLEDGE BOX.

INEXPRESSIBLES. Breeches.

A Foul Emission

BROTHER ROUND MOUTH SPEAKS

CHEESER

FIZZLE

FOYSE

ICE

INKLE WEAVERS. Supposed to be a very brotherly set of people; 'as great as two inkle weavers' being a proverbial saying.

IRON. Money in general. To polish the king's iron with one's eyebrows; to look out of grated or prison windows.

ISLAND. He drank out of the bottle till he saw the island; the island is the rising bottom of a wine bottle, which appears like an island in the centre, before the bottle is quite empty.

IVORIES. Teeth. How the swell flashed his ivories; how the gentleman shewed his teeth.

PLATE XIII

Island

J.

JACKEY. Gin.

JAW. Speech, discourse. Give us none of your jaw; let us have none of your discourse. A jaw-me-dead; a talkative fellow. Jaw work; a cry used in fairs by the sellers of nuts.

JESUIT. *See* TO BOX THE JESUIT.

JINGLE BRAINS. A wild, thoughtless, rattling fellow.

JOBBERNOLE. The head.

TO JOCK, or JOCKUM CLOY. To enjoy a woman.

JOLLY, or JOLLY NOB. The head. I'll lump your jolly nob for you; I'll give you a knock on the head.

JOLLY DOG. A merry facetious fellow; a bon vivant, who never flinches from his glass, nor cries to go home to bed.

JUST-ASS. A punning appellation for a justice.

K.

TO KEEP IT UP. To prolong a debauch. We kept it up finely last night; metaphor drawn from the game of shuttle-cock.

KETTLE OF FISH. When a person has perplexed his affairs in general, or any particular business, he is said to have made a fine kettle of fish of it.

KETTLEDRUMS. Cupid's kettle-drums; a woman's breasts, called by sailors chest and bedding.

KICKS. Breeches. A high kick; the top of the fashion. It is all the kick; it is the present mode. A kick in the guts; a dram of gin, or any other spirituous liquor. A kick up; a disturbance, also a hop or dance. An odd kick in one's gallop; a strange whim or peculiarity.

KILL DEVIL. New still-burnt rum.

KILL PRIEST. Port wine.

KING'S BAD BARGAIN. One of the king's bad bargains; a malingeror, or soldier who shirks his duty.

KING'S PICTURES. Coin, money.

Female Naughty Bits: Above

APPLE
DUMPLIN SHOP

A BUSHEL BUBBY

CAT-HEADS

DAIRY

DIDDEYS

DUGS

HEAVERS

KETTLEDRUMS

KNOB. The head. *See* NOB.

KNOCK. To knock a woman; to have carnal knowledge of her. To knock off; to conclude: phrase borrowed from the blacksmith.

KNOWLEDGE BOX. The head.

L.

LADY DACRE'S WINE. Gin.

LADYBIRDS. Light or lewd women.

LARK. A piece of merriment. People playing together jocosely.

LAUGH. To laugh on the wrong side of the mouth; to cry. I'll make him laugh on the wrong [or t'other] side of his mouth.

LAUNCH. The delivery, or labour, of a pregnant woman.

LAWFUL BLANKET. A wife.

LAZY MAN'S LOAD. Lazy people frequently take up more than they can safely carry, to save the trouble of coming a second time.

LEAKY. Apt to blab; one who cannot keep a secret is said to be leaky.

TO LIB. To lie together.

LICKSPITTLE. A parasite, or tale-bearer.

LIFT. To give one a lift; to assist. A good hand at a dead lift; a good hand upon an emergency. To lift one's hand to one's

PLATE XIV

Lawful Blanket

head; to drink to excess, or to drink drams. To lift or raise one's elbow; the same.

LIGHT HOUSE. A man with a red fiery nose.

LIGHTNING. Gin. A flash of lightning; a glass of gin.

LIMBS. Duke of limbs; a tall awkward fellow.

LIQUOR. To liquor one's boots; to drink before a journey.

LOAF. To be in bad loaf, to be in a disagreeable situation, or in trouble.

LONG STOMACH. A voracious appetite.

LOUSE. A gentleman's companion. He will never louse a grey head of his own; he will never live to be old.

LOW TIDE, or LOW WATER. When there is no money in a man's pocket.

LUGS. Ears or wattles. *See* WATTLES.

LULLABY CHEAT. An infant.

LURCH. To be left in the lurch; to be abandoned by one's confederates or party, to be left in a scrape.

M.

MADE. Stolen.

MADGE. The private parts of a woman.

MALKIN, or MAULKIN. A general name for a cat; also a parcel of rags fastened to the end of a stick, to clean an oven.

MAN TRAP. A woman's commodity.

MARE'S NEST. He has found a mare's nest, and is laughing at the eggs; said of one who laughs without any apparent cause.

MARRIAGE MUSIC. The squalling and crying of children.

MASTER OF THE WARDROBE. One who pawns his clothes to purchase liquor.

MAULED. Extremely drunk, or soundly beaten.

MAWLEY. A hand. Tip us your mawley; shake hands with me. Fam the mawley; shake hands.

MAX. Gin.

Hands

DADDLES

FAMBLES

FAMS

FOREFEET

MAWLEYS

MAY BEES. May bees don't fly all the year long; an answer to any one who prefaces a proposition with, It may be.

MELLOW. Almost drunk.

TO MILK THE PIGEON. To endeavour at impossibilities.

MISS LAYCOCK. The monosyllable.

MONKEY. To suck the monkey; to suck or draw wine, or any other liquor, privately out of a cask, by means of a straw.

MONOSYLLABLE. A woman's commodity.

TO MOP UP. To drink up. To empty a glass or pot.

PLATE XV

Milk the Pigeon

MORE-ISH. This wine has but one fault, and that is, it is more-ish: *i.e.*, more of it is wanted, or there is too little of it.

MORT. A woman or wench.

MOSSY FACE. The mother of all saints.

MOTHER OF ALL SAINTS. The monosyllable.

MOTHER OF ALL SOULS. The same.

MOTHER OF ST. PATRICK. The same.

MOUSE. To speak like a mouse in a cheese; *i.e.*, faintly or indistinctly.

MOUSETRAP. The parson's mouse-trap; the state of matrimony.

MOVEABLES. Rings, watches, or any toys of value.

MUCK. Money; also dung.

MUFF. The private parts of a woman. To the well wearing of your muff, mort; to the happy consummation of your marriage, girl; a health.

MUFFLING CHEAT. A napkin.

MUMMER. The mouth.

MUSHROOM. A person or family suddenly raised to riches and eminence: an allusion to that fungus, which starts up in a night.

MUTTON. In her mutton, *i.e.,* having carnal knowledge of a woman.

MUZZLE. A beard.

N.

NACKY. Ingenious.

NAPPER OF NAPS. A sheep stealer.

NAPPER. The head; also a cheat or thief.

NAZY. Drunken. Nazy cove or mort; a drunken rogue or harlot. Nazy nabs; drunken coxcombs.

NICK NINNY. A simpleton.

Not Very Bright

ADDLE PATE

BIRD-WITTED

BOTTLE-HEADED

BUFFLE-HEADED

CHUCKLE-HEADED

CLUNCH

CORK-BRAINED

FLATT

FRIG PIG

JINGLE BRAINS

NICK NINNY

NIFFYNAFFY

NINNYHAMMER

PUDDING-HEADED

RATTLE-PATE

SHALLOW PATE

NICKNACKS. Toys, baubles, or curiosities.

NIFFYNAFFY FELLOW. A trifler.

NINE LIVES. Cats are said to have nine lives, and women ten cats' lives.

NINNY, or NINNYHAMMER. A simpleton.

NIX. Nothing.

NOB. The head.

NOD. He is gone to the land of Nod; he is asleep.

NODDLE. The head.

NOPE. A blow: as, I took him a nope on the costard.

NOTCH. The private parts of a woman.

NOZZLE. The nose of a man or woman.

NUB. The neck; also coition.

NUG. An endearing word: as, My dear nug; my dear love.

NUTMEGS. Testicles.

NUTS. It was nuts for them; *i.e.,* it was very agreeable to them.

PLATE XVI

Nutmegs

O.

OAR. To put in one's oar; to intermeddle, or give an opinion unasked.

OATS. He has sowed his wild oats; he is staid, or sober, having left off his wild tricks.

OCCUPY. To occupy a woman; to have carnal knowledge of her.

ODD-COME-SHORTLYS. I'll do it one of these odd-come-shortlys; I will do it some time or another.

OGLES. Eyes. Rum ogles; fine eyes.

OIL OF BARLEY, or BARLEY BROTH. Strong beer.

OLD DOG AT IT. Expert, accustomed.

ONE OF US, or ONE OF MY COUSINS. A woman of the town, a harlot.

ORGAN. A pipe. Will you cock your organ? Will you smoke your pipe?

OTTOMISED. To be ottomised; to be dissected. You'll be scragged, ottomised, and grin in a glass case: you'll be hanged, anatomised, and your skeleton kept in a glass case at Surgeons' Hall.

PLATE XVII

Organ

OUTRUN THE CONSTABLE.
A man who has lived above his means, or income, is said to have outrun the constable.

OWL IN AN IVY BUSH. He looks like an owl in an ivy bush; frequently said of a person with a large frizzled wig, or a woman whose hair is dressed a-la-blowze.

P.

PAD BORROWERS. Horse stealers.

PARENTHESIS. To put a man's nose into a parenthesis: to pull it, the fingers and thumb answering the hooks or crochets. A wooden parenthesis; the pillory. An iron parenthesis; a prison.

PARK PAILING. Teeth.

PATE. The head. Carroty-pated; red-haired.

TO PEEL. To strip: allusion to taking off the coat or rind of an orange or apple.

PEEPERS. Eyes. Single peeper, a one-eyed man.

PEEPY. Drowsy.

PEGO. The penis of man or beast.

PELT. A heat, chase, or passion: as, What a pelt he was in!

PET. In a pet; in a passion or miff.

PHARAOH. Strong malt liquor.

PHILISTINES. Bailiffs, or officers of justice; also drunkards.

PILGRIM'S SALVE. A sirreverence, human excrement.

PIN. In or to a merry pin; almost drunk: an allusion to a sort of tankard, formerly used in the north, having silver pegs or pins set at equal distances from the top to the bottom: by the rules of good fellowship, every person drinking out of one of these tankards, was to swallow the quantity contained between two pins; if he drank more or less, he was to continue drinking till he ended at a pin.

PISSING DOWN ANY ONE'S BACK. Flattering him.

PITCHER. The miraculous pitcher, that holds water with the mouth downwards: a woman's commodity.

Almost Drunk

———

A DROP IN
THE EYE

HALF SEAS OVER

HICKEY

IN A MERRY PIN

MELLOW

TIPSEY

PLATE. Money, silver, prize.

PLUG TAIL. A man's penis.

PLUMP CURRANT. I am not plump currant; I am out of sorts.

POGY. Drunk.

POISONED. Big with child: that wench is poisoned.

POTATOE TRAP. The mouth. Shut your potatoe trap and give your tongue a holiday; *i.e.,* be silent.

PRATING CHEAT. The tongue.

PRATTLE BROTH. Tea. *See* CHATTER BROTH, SCANDAL BROTH, &c.

PRATTS. Buttocks; also a tinder box.

PLATE XVIII

Pogy

PRAY. She prays with her knees upwards; said of a woman much given to gallantry and intrigue.

PRIGGING. Riding; also lying with a woman.

PROUD. Desirous of copulation.

PUDDING SLEEVES. A parson.

PUDDING-HEADED FELLOW. A stupid fellow, one whose brains are all in confusion.

PUDDINGS. The guts: I'll let out your puddings.

PULL. To be pulled; to be arrested by a police officer. To have a pull is to have an advantage; generally where a person has some superiority at a game of chance or skill.

PULLY HAWLY. To have a game at pully hawly; to romp with women.

PUZZLE-TEXT. An ignorant blundering parson.

Q.

QUACKING CHEAT. A duck.

QUAIL-PIPE. A woman's tongue; also a device to take birds of that name by imitating their call.

QUIDS. Cash, money. Can you tip me any quids? Can you lend me some money?

QUIFFING. Rogering. *See* TO ROGER.

R.

RABBIT CATCHER. A midwife.

RAG. Bank notes. Money in general. The cove has no rag; the fellow has no money.

RAG WATER. Gin, or any other common dram: these liquors seldom failing to reduce those that drink them to rags.

PLATE XIX

Rabbit Catcher

RAMMER. The arm. The busnapper's kenchin seized my rammer; *i.e.,* the watchman laid hold of my arm.

RANTALLION. One whose scrotum is so relaxed as to be longer than his penis, *i.e.,* whose shot pouch is longer than the barrel of his piece.

RANTUM SCANTUM. Playing at rantum scantum; making the beast with two backs.

RATTLE-PATE. A volatile, unsteady, or whimsical man or woman.

READY. The ready rhino; money.

RECEIVER GENERAL. A prostitute.

RECKON. To reckon with one's host; to make an erroneous judgment in one's own favour. To cast-up one's reckoning or accounts; to vomit.

RED LANE. The throat. Gone down the red lane; swallowed.

RED RAG. The tongue. Shut your potatoe trap, and give your red rag a holiday; *i.e.,* shut your mouth, and let your tongue rest. Too much of the red rag [too much tongue].

RED RIBBIN. Brandy.

RHINO. Money.

RIB. A wife: an allusion to our common mother Eve, made out of Adam's rib. A crooked rib; a cross-grained wife.

Vomit

———

CASCADE

CASTING UP ONE'S
ACCOUNTS

TO CAT, OR
SHOOT THE CAT

FLASH THE HASH

FLAY THE FOX

RECKON

SH-T-NG THROUGH
THE TEETH

RIBBIN. Money. The ribbin runs thick; *i.e.*, there is plenty of money. Blue ribbin. Gin. The cull lushes the blue ribbin; the silly fellow drinks common gin.

TO RIBROAST. To beat: I'll ribroast him to his heart's content.

RIDING ST. GEORGE. The woman uppermost in the amorous congress, that is, the dragon upon St. George.

TO ROGER. To bull, or lie with a woman; from the name of Roger being frequently given to a bull.

ROPES. Upon the high ropes; elated, in high spirits, cock-a-hoop.

ROUND MOUTH. The fundament. Brother round mouth speaks; he has let a fart.

RUFFLES. Handcuffs.

RUG. Asleep. The whole gill is safe at rug; the people of the house are fast asleep.

RUM. Fine, good, valuable.

RUM BLOWER. A handsome wench.

RUM BLUFFER. A jolly host.

RUM BUGHER. A valuable dog.

RUM BUNG. A full purse.

RUM DOXY. A fine wench.

RUM DUKE. A jolly handsome fellow.

RUM NAB. A good hat.

RUM PEEPERS. Fine looking-glasses.

RUM PRANCER. A fine horse.

RUM SQUEEZE. Much wine, or good liquor, given among fiddlers.

RUMBO. Rum, water, and sugar; also a prison.

S.

SACK. A pocket. To buy the sack: to get drunk. To dive into the sack; to pick a pocket. To break a bottle in an empty sack; a bubble bet, a sack with a bottle in it not being an empty sack.

SAINT GEOFFREY'S DAY. Never, there being no saint of that name: tomorrow-come-never, when two Sundays come together.

PLATE XX

Sea Lawyer

SCANDAL BROTH. Tea.

SCAPEGRACE. A wild dissolute fellow.

SCRUBBADO. The itch.

SEA CRAB. A sailor.

SEA LAWYER. A shark.

SEES. The eyes. *See* DAY LIGHTS.

TO SETTLE. To knock down or stun any one. We settled the cull by a stroke on his nob; we stunned the fellow by a blow on the head.

SHALLOW PATE. A simple fellow.

SHEEP'S HEAD. Like a sheep's head, all jaw; saying of a talkative man or woman.

SHILLY-SHALLY. Irresolute. To stand shilly-shally; to hesitate, or stand in doubt.

SH-T SACK. A dastardly fellow: also a non-conformist.

SH-T-NG THROUGH THE TEETH. Vomiting. Hark ye, friend, have you got a padlock on your a-se, that you sh-te through your teeth? Vulgar address to one vomiting.

TO SHOOT THE CAT. To vomit from excess of liquor; called also catting.

SHOULDER FEAST. A dinner given after a funeral, to those who have carried the corpse.

PLATE XXI

To Shoot the Cat

SHOVEL. To be put to bed with a shovel; to be buried. He or she was fed with a fire-shovel; a saying of a person with a large mouth.

SIDE POCKET. He has as much need of a wife as a dog of a side pocket; said of a weak old debilitated man. He wants it as much as a dog does a side pocket; a simile used for one who desires any thing by no means necessary.

SILENT FLUTE. *See* PEGO, SUGAR STICK, &c.

TO SING SMALL. To be humbled, confounded, or abashed, to have little or nothing to say for one's-self.

SIR REVERENCE. Human excrement, a t--d.

SKY BLUE. Gin.

SLEEPY. Much worn; the cloth of your coat must be extremely sleepy, for it has not had a nap this long time.

SLICE. To take a slice; to intrigue, particularly with a married woman, because a slice off a cut loaf is not missed.

SLUG-A-BED. A drone, one that cannot rise in the morning.

SLUICE YOUR GOB. Take a hearty drink.

SLUSH BUCKET. A foul feeder, one that eats much greasy food.

SLY BOOTS. A cunning fellow, under the mask of simplicity.

SMELLER. A nose. Smellers: a cat's whiskers.

SMITER. An arm. To smite one's tutor; to get money from him.

TO SNABBLE. To rifle or plunder; also to kill.

TO SNAFFLE. To steal. To snaffle any one's poll; to steal his wig.

SNAFFLER. A highwayman. Snaffler of prances; a horse stealer.

SNAGGS. Large teeth; also snails.

SNEAKSBY. A mean-spirited fellow, a sneaking cur.

TO SNILCH. To eye, or look at any thing attentively: the cull snilches.

SNUG. All's snug; all's quiet.

TO SOAK. To drink. An old soaker; a drunkard, one that moistens his clay to make it stick together.

SOLO PLAYER. A miserable performer on any instrument, who always plays alone, because no one will stay in the room to hear him.

SON OF PRATTLEMENT. A lawyer.

SOUTH SEA. Gin.

SPANKS, or SPANKERS. Money.

TO SPEAK WITH. To rob. I spoke with the cull on the cherry-coloured prancer; I robbed the man on the black horse.

Gin

BLUE RIBBIN

BLUE RUIN

DIDDLE

DRAIN

FROG'S WINE

HEART'S EASE

JACKEY

KICK

LADY DACRE'S
WINE

LIGHTNING

MAX

RAG WATER

SKY BLUE

SOUTH SEA

STRIP ME NAKED

TAPE

WHITE RIBBIN

TO SPIFLICATE. To confound, silence, or dumbfound.

SPLICED. Married: an allusion to joining two ropes ends by splicing.

SQUEEZE CRAB. A sour-looking, shrivelled, diminutive fellow.

STAMPERS. Shoes.

STAMPS. Legs.

STEPHEN. Money. Stephen's at home; *i.e.*, has money.

STICK FLAMS. A pair of gloves.

STIFF-RUMPED. Proud, stately.

STIRRUP CUP. A parting cup or glass, drank on horseback by the person taking leave.

STRAPPING. Lying with a woman.

STRIP ME NAKED. Gin.

TO STRUM. To have carnal knowledge of a woman; also to play badly on the harpsichord.

STUBBLE IT. Hold your tongue.

STUMPS. Legs. To stir one's stumps; to walk fast.

SUCK. Strong liquor of any sort. To suck the monkey; *see* MONKEY. Sucky; drunk.

SUGAR STICK. The virile member.

SUN. To have been in the sun; said of one that is drunk.

SUNBURNT. Clapped; also having many male children.

SURVEYOR OF THE HIGH-WAYS. One reeling drunk.

SWILL TUB. A drunkard, a sot.

TO SWIVE. To copulate.

SWIZZLE. Drink, or any brisk or windy liquor.

T.

TALLYWAGS, OR TARRYWAGS. A man's testicles.

TAPE. Red, white, or blue tape; gin, or any other spirituous liquor.

TARADIDDLE. A fib, or falsity.

TEARS OF THE TANKARD. The drippings of liquor on a man's waistcoat.

Male Naughty Bits: The Pair

BAWBLES

CODS

GINGAMBOBS

NUTMEGS

TALLYWAGS

THINGAMABOBS

TWIDDLE-DIDDLES

WHIRLYGIGS

THIEF. You are a thief and a murderer, you have killed a baboon and stole his face; vulgar abuse.

THINGAMABOBS. Testicles.

THOMAS. Man Thomas; a man's penis.

TIBBY. A cat.

TICKLE PITCHER. A thirsty fellow, a sot.

TICKLE TAIL. A rod, or schoolmaster. A man's penis.

TIFFING. Eating or drinking out of meal time, disputing or falling out; also lying with a wench.

TO TIP. To give or lend. Tip me your daddle; give me your hand. Tip me a hog; give me a shilling.

PLATE XXII

Tiffing

TIPPLE. Liquor.

TIPPLERS. Sots who are continually
sipping.

TIPSEY. Almost drunk.

TOASTING IRON, or CHEESE
TOASTER. A sword.

TOGS. Clothes. The swell is rum-togged.
The gentleman is handsomely dressed.

TOM LONG. A tiresome story teller. It
is coming by Tom Long, the carrier; said
of any thing that has been long expected.

TONGUE. Tongue enough for two sets
of teeth: said of a talkative person. As old
as my tongue, and a little older than my
teeth; a dovetail in answer to the question, How old are you?

TOOLS. The private parts of a man.

TOOTH MUSIC. Chewing.

TOP HEAVY. Drunk.

TOP LIGHTS. The eyes.

TORMENTER OF CATGUT. A fiddler.

TORMENTER OF SHEEP SKIN. A drummer.

TOSS OFF. Manual pollution.

TOSS POT. A drunkard.

TROTTERS. Feet.

TRUNK. A nose. To shove a trunk: to introduce one's self unasked into any place or company.

Male Naughty Bits:
The Altogether

———

BARBER'S SIGN

TOOLS

TUZZY-MUZZY. The monosyllable.

TWIDDLE-DIDDLES. Testicles.

TO TWIG. To observe. Twig the cull, he is peery; observe the fellow, he is watching us.

TWO HANDED PUT. The amorous congress.

U.

UNICORN. A coach drawn by three horses.

UPPER STORY, or GARRET. Figuratively used to signify the head. His upper story or garrets are unfurnished; *i.e.,* he is an empty or foolish fellow.

V.

VICE ADMIRAL OF THE
NARROW SEAS. A drunken man
that pisses under the table into his companions' shoes.

VICTUALLING OFFICE. The
stomach.

W.

TO WAP. To copulate.

WARE. A woman's ware; her commodity.

WATERY-HEADED. Apt to shed tears.

WATTLES. Ears.

WHIFFLES. A relaxation of the scrotum.

Amorous Congress

AT CLICKET

BASKET-MAKING

BLANKET HORNPIPE

BLOWING THE
GROUNSILS

BUTTOCK BALL

DOCKING

FACE-MAKING

FLOURISHING

GIVING A
GREEN GOWN

HUMPING

JOCKING

JOINING GIBLETS

KNOCKING

LIBBING

NUBBING

OCCUPYING

PLAYING AT
RANTUM SCANTUM

PRIGGING

QUIFFING

RIDING
ST. GEORGE

ROGERING

STRAPPING

STRUMMING

SWIVING

TAKING A FLYER

TAKING A SLICE

TIFFING

WAPPING

WHIRLYGIGS. Testicles.

WHISKER. A great lie.

WHISKER SPLITTER. A man of intrigue.

WHITE RIBBIN. Gin.

WHITHER-GO-YE. A wife: wives being sometimes apt to question their husbands whither they are going.

WIBBLE. Bad drink.

WIGSBY. Mr. Wigsby; a man wearing a wig.

WOMBLETY CROPT. The indisposition of a drunkard after a debauch.

WOOL GATHERING. Your wits are gone a woolgathering; saying to an absent man, one in a reverie, or absorbed in thought.

WOOLBIRD. A sheep.

WORD PECKER. A punster, one who plays upon words.

WRAPT UP IN WARM FLAN-NEL. Drunk with spirituous liquors.

Y.

YAFFLING. Eating.

Library of Congress
Cataloging-in-Publication Data available.
ISBN 978-1-4521-8460-9

Manufactured in China.

Design by Liam Flanagan.
Illustrations by Johnny Sampson.
10 9 8 7 6 5 4 3 2

Chronicle books and gifts are available at special quantity
discounts to corporations, professional associations,
literacy programs, and other organizations. For details
and discount information, please contact our premiums
department at corporatesales@chroniclebooks.com or at
1-800-759-0190.

Chronicle Books LLC
680 Second Street
San Francisco, California 94107
www.chroniclebooks.com